THE FINAL FOUR

BY ELLIOTT SMITH

Apex is distributed by North Star Editions:
sales@northstareditions.com | 888-417-0195

Produced for Apex by Red Line Editorial.

Photographs ©: Brynn Anderson/AP Images, cover; David J. Phillip/AP Images, 4–5, 6–7, 8–9, 29; NCAA Photos/Getty Images, 10–11; Bob Jordan/AP Images, 12–13; Eric Draper/AP Images, 14–15; Shutterstock Images, 1, 16–17, 18–19, 20–21, 22–23, 24–25; Bailey Hillesheim/Icon Sportswire/AP Images, 27

Library of Congress Control Number: 2022912153

ISBN
978-1-63738-292-9 (hardcover)
978-1-63738-328-5 (paperback)
978-1-63738-398-8 (ebook pdf)
978-1-63738-364-3 (hosted ebook)

Printed in the United States of America
Mankato, MN
012023

NOTE TO PARENTS AND EDUCATORS

Apex books are designed to build literacy skills in striving readers. Exciting, high-interest content attracts and holds readers' attention. The text is carefully leveled to allow students to achieve success quickly. Additional features, such as bolded glossary words for difficult terms, help build comprehension.

TABLE OF CONTENTS

CHAPTER 1

THE COMEBACK

The North Carolina Tar Heels are facing the Kansas Jayhawks. They are playing in the 2022 Final Four **championship**. The Tar Heels start strong. They build a lead of 16 points.

Kansas's Jalen Wilson (left) takes a shot during the 2022 Final Four championship.

But Kansas takes control in the second half. Nearly 10 minutes in, the game is tied. Then Kansas gains the lead with a three-pointer!

A TALE OF TWO HALVES

In the first half, North Carolina scored 40 points. Kansas scored just 25. But in the second half, Kansas scored 47 points. North Carolina managed only 29.

Remy Martin (11) shoots during the 2022 championship.

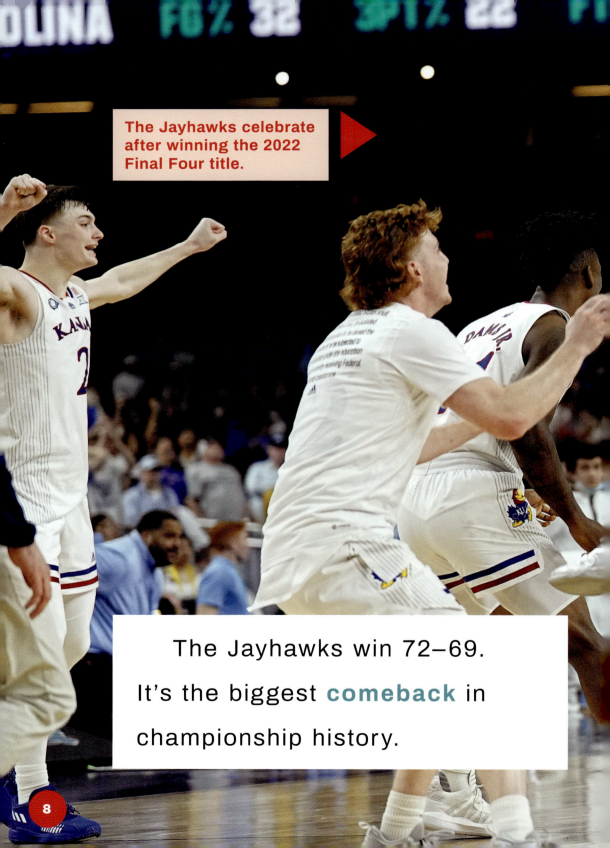

The Jayhawks celebrate after winning the 2022 Final Four title.

The Jayhawks win 72–69. It's the biggest **comeback** in championship history.

FAST FACT

The Tar Heels nearly tied the game at the buzzer. But they missed a three-pointer.

CHAPTER 2

NCAA HISTORY

The Final Four is part of a **tournament** held by the National Collegiate Athletic Association (NCAA). The first tournament was in 1939. Eight teams played.

An Oregon player (18) defends during the 1939 NCAA championship. Oregon ended up winning.

Over time, more teams took part. There were 16 teams in 1951. As of 2022, 68 teams were playing.

FAST FACT

The NCAA tournament is also called March Madness. People started using this name in the 1980s.

Michael Jordan (23) led North Carolina to a championship in 1982.

In 1995, the UCLA Bruins won their 11th NCAA title.

Teams try to reach the last game and win the **title**. Great teams do this many times. The UCLA Bruins once won seven titles in a row.

THE FIRST WOMEN'S TITLE

For decades, only men could reach the Final Four. That changed in 1982. That year, the NCAA began having a women's tournament, too. Louisiana Tech won.

CHAPTER 3

REACHING THE FINAL FOUR

There are two ways to play in the NCAA tournament. Some teams **qualify** by winning their **conference** tournaments. A group of experts pick the rest.

In the 2010s, the Arizona Wildcats reached the finals of their conference tournament six times.

Teams are placed in a **bracket**. The best teams get No. 1 **seeds**. The biggest **underdogs** get No. 16 seeds.

The Final Four is usually played in a large stadium.

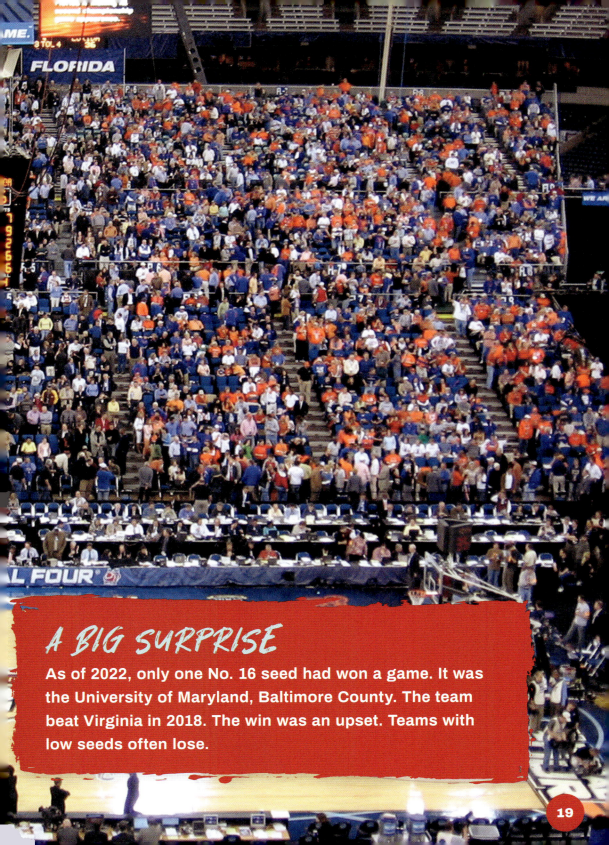

A BIG SURPRISE

As of 2022, only one No. 16 seed had won a game. It was the University of Maryland, Baltimore County. The team beat Virginia in 2018. The win was an upset. Teams with low seeds often lose.

| FIRST ROUND MARCH 20 | SECOND ROUND MARCH 22 | SWEET 16 MARCH 27-28 | ELITE 8' MARCH 29-30 | NATIONAL SEMIFINALS APRIL 3 |

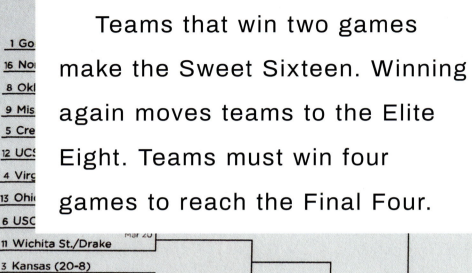

Teams that win two games make the Sweet Sixteen. Winning again moves teams to the Elite Eight. Teams must win four games to reach the Final Four.

1 Go
16 Nor
8 Okl
9 Mis
5 Cre
12 UCS
4 Virg
13 Ohi
6 USC
11 Wichita St./Drake
3 Kansas (20-8)
14 Eastern Wash. (16-7)   Mar 20
7 Oregon (20-6)
10 VCU (19-7)   Mar 20
2 Iowa (21-8)
15 Grand Can

1 Michig
16 Mt. S
8 LSU
9 St. E
5 Color
12 George
4 Florida S
13 UNC Greensb
6 BYU (20-6)
11 Michigan St./UCLA   Mar 20
3 Texas (19-7)
14 Abilene Christian (23-4)   Mar 20
7 UConn (15-7)
10 Maryland (16-13)   Mar 20

FAST FACT

People often fill out March Madness brackets. They guess the winner for each game.

ASKETBALL CHAMPIONSHIP

R"

E | Mount St. Mary's (12-10) 16
Mar 18
Texas Southern (16-8) 16

E | Michigan St. (15-12) 11
Mar 18
UCLA (17-9) 11

Baylor (22-2) 1
Mar 19
Hartford (15-8) 16

North Carolina (18-10) 8
Mar 19
Wisconsin (17-12) 9

Villanova (16-6) 5
Mar 19
Winthrop (23-1) 12

Purdue (18-9) 4
Mar 19
North Texas (17-9) 13

SOUTH

Texas Tech (17-10) 6
Mar 19
Utah St. (20-8) 11

Arkansas (22-6) 3
Mar 19
Colgate (14-1) 14

Florida (14-9) 7
Mar 19
Virginia Tech (15-6) 10

Ohio St. (21-9) 2
Mar 19
Oral Roberts (16-10) 15

HIP

SEMIFINALS

Illinois (23-6) 1
Mar 19
Drexel (12-7) 16

Loyola Chicago (24-4) 8
Mar 19
Georgia Tech (17-8) 9

> **Some people fill out paper March Madness brackets. Others fill them out online.**

Tennessee (18-8) 5
Mar 19
Oregon St. (17-12) 12

Oklahoma St. (20-8) 4
Mar 19
Liberty (23-5) 13

San Diego St. (23-4) 6
Mar 19
Syracuse (16-9) 11

West Virginia (18-9) 3
Mar 19
Morehead St. (23-7) 14

MIDWEST

Clemson (16-7) 7
Mar 19
Rutgers (15-11) 1

Houston (24-3) 2

ESS

works
DNESS

21

cHAMPiONS!

Final Four history is filled with great champions. Connecticut's women's team is among the best. The Huskies won four straight titles from 2013 to 2016.

Connecticut Huskies center Kiah Stokes passes the ball during a 2013 game.

In 2022, the Tar Heels men's team made its 21st Final Four. That was the most ever. Kentucky, Kansas, UCLA, and Duke had also made many Final Fours.

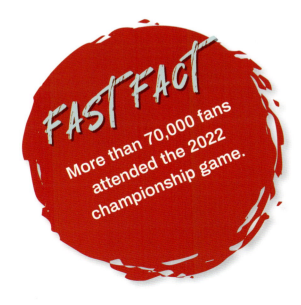

FAST FACT

More than 70,000 fans attended the 2022 championship game.

Pat Summitt (left) coached Tennessee's women's team to eight titles. Mike Krzyzewski coached Duke's men's team to five.

Villanova won the men's title in 2016 and 2018. South Carolina won the women's championship in 2022. That was the team's second title in five tournaments.

CUTTING THE NET

Every year, championship players climb a tall ladder. Then they cut down the net. Each member of the team gets to keep a piece.

Aliyah Boston cuts the net after leading South Carolina to the 2022 NCAA title.

COMPREHENSION QUESTIONS

Write your answers on a separate piece of paper.

1. Write a paragraph that explains the path teams must take to reach the Final Four.

2. Would you want to play in the Final Four? Why or why not?

3. In 2022, how many teams played in the NCAA tournament?

    A. 8

    B. 16

    C. 68

4. In what year could women's teams first reach the Final Four?

    A. 1939

    B. 1982

    C. 2022

5. What does **managed** mean in this book?

But in the second half, Kansas scored
47 points. North Carolina managed only 29.

    A. scored

    B. shouted

    C. was in charge

6. What does **upset** mean in this book?

The win was an upset. Teams with low seeds
often lose.

    A. an event that often happens

    B. an event that is not real

    C. an event that is a surprise

Answer key on page 32.

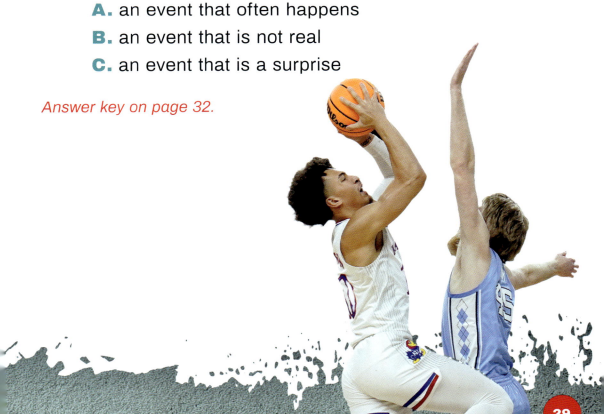

GLOSSARY

bracket

A diagram that represents a series of games to be played.

championship

The final game that decides the winner of a tournament.

comeback

A situation in which a team is losing but ends up taking the lead.

conference

A smaller group of teams within a sports league.

qualify

To make it into a competition.

seeds

The places teams are ranked for a tournament.

title

The top finish in a sports competition.

tournament

A competition that includes several teams.

underdogs

Teams that are not expected to win.

TO LEARN MORE

BOOKS

Morey, Allan. *The Final Four*. Minneapolis: Bellwether Media, 2019.

Omoth, Tyler. *College Basketball's Championship*. North Mankato, MN: Capstone Press, 2018.

Williamson, Ryan. *College Basketball Hot Streaks*. Mankato, MN: The Child's World, 2019.

ONLINE RESOURCES

Visit **www.apexeditions.com** to find links and resources related to this title.

ABOUT THE AUTHOR

Elliott Smith lives in Falls Church, Virginia. He enjoys watching movies, reading, and playing sports with his two children. His favorite college basketball team has made the NCAA tournament only one time.

INDEX

ANSWER KEY:
1. Answers will vary; 2. Answers will vary; 3. C; 4. B; 5. A; 6. C